The Qin Dynasty Terra-Cotta Army of
Dreams

Queen Elizabeth II of the United Kingdom   October 16 th,1986

American President Bill Clinton   June 26 th，1998

President of the Russian Federation Vladimir Putin   October 16 th, 2004

His Majesty Albert II, King of the Belgians   June 8th, 2005

The Qin Dynasty Terra-Cotta Army of Dreams

CONTENTS

Emperor Qin's Terra-cotta Museum- The Biggest On-site Museum in China

The well-known Terra-cotta Museum is located on the east side of the Mausoleum of Emperor QinShihuang, the first emperor in Chinese history. The Museum covers a total area of 20 hectares. It is decorated with verdant trees, blooming flowers and green grass. It is a delightful scene. Three main buildings of the museum named Pit 1, Pit 2 and Pit 3 were constructed on the original site of the pits at different times.

On March 29,1974, local farmers of XiYang village, LingTong County, were drilling a series of wells in search of water. They discovered some pottery fragments and ancient bronze weapons. The head of the village reported the news to the local government at once. The news aroused much attention from both local Government and National Historical &Cultural Relics Administration. With government approval, an archaeological team from Shaanxi Province arrived at the site on July 17, 1974 and began their explorations and excavations. On October 1st, 1979 Emperor QinShihuang's Terra-cotta Museum was opened to the public. By the time of the opening ceremony, archaeologists had excavated an area of 2,000 square meters in Pit No.1 and some 1,087 terra-cotta warriors and horses were displayed there after restoration. The village, formerly unknown to the outside world, has become world famous.

The archaeological wonders discovered here came as a shock to China and the world. Following the discovery of Pit No.1, Pit No.2 and Pit No.3 were unearthed in April and May of 1976. Pit No.3 was opened to the public in 1989. Excavation of Pit 2 began in March 1994 and it was opened in October of the same year while still being excavated. In addition to the three pits, two sets of bronze chariots and horses were discovered on the west side of Emperor Qin's mausoleum in December 1980. These were displayed in the museum after restoration.

In the last 20 years, the terra-cotta museum has become the largest on-site museum in China. The staff of the museum has increased. More and more valuable cultural relics have been unearthed.

Pit No.1 is a huge arch-domed steel structure, located at the center of the museum with an area of 16,000 square meters. Pit 2 and 3, built in Qin and Han Dynasty tomb mound style cover an area of 17,934 and 1,694 square meters respectively. Multiple exhibition building, to the east of Pit 2, covers an area of 7,100 square meters. They provide a series of exhibits, including the bronze chariots and horses, the new findings from the Emperor Qin's Mausoleum, the history of the museum and various temporary exhibits. These displays depict the history of the Qin Dynasty and help the viewers get a better understanding of the Terra-cotta Warriors and Horses. South of Pit 1 is the circle vision hall. The movie, lasting 20 minutes, vividly tells the story of the reign of Emperor Qin and the construction and subsequent destruction of his terra-cotta army 2,200 years ago. Halls on the northwest side of Pit 3, covering 4,282 square meters, are multiple service halls where visitors can eat, shop or rest.

Emperor Qin's Terra-cotta Museum is not only a treasure house where tourists can learn about Chinese history and culture but also a main scenic area for Xi'an city. It receives 2 million tourists annually. 50 million visitors from home and abroad have visited the museum in the last 20 years. Today the description, "Eighth Wonder of the world" has almost become synonymous with the Terra-cotta Museum. In 1987 the Emperor Qin's mausoleum was placed on UNESCO list as a world-class cultural heritage site. The Museum is widely known as a huge modern on-site museum that is going to be one of the best in the world.

The multiple service halls

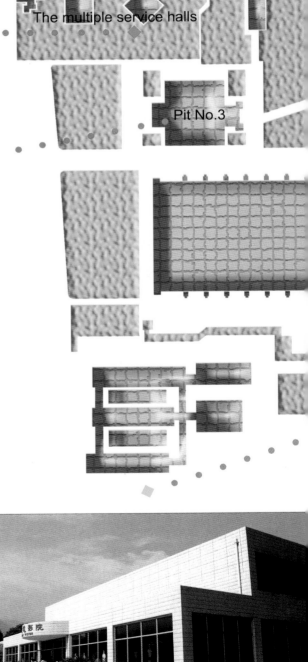

The multiple service halls

Pit No.3

Pit No.3

The circle vision hall

Pit No.2

N

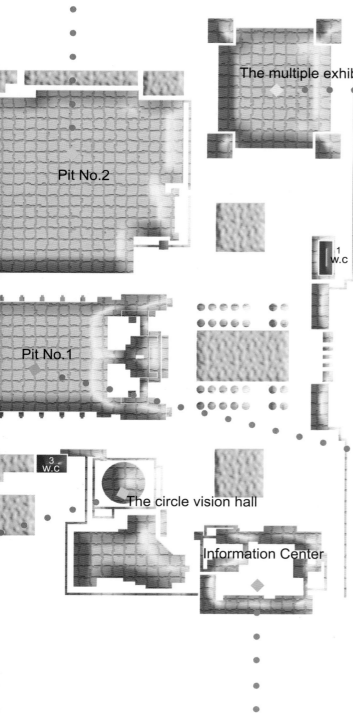

The multiple exhibition building

Pit No.2

Pit No.1

1
w.c

3
W.C

The circle vision hall

Information Center

Information Center

The multiple exhibition building

Pit No.1

Emperor QinShihuang - the First Emperor in Chinese History

Many important men have crossed the Chinese historical stage in the last 5,000 years. Emperor QinShihuang, the first emperor in Chinese history, was one of the most important. He was born the son of King ZhuangXiang, the King of Qin, in the first month of the lunar year in 259 BC. Initially named ZhaoZheng, his name was later changed to YingZheng.

YingZheng's mother was a beautiful concubine of Lu Buwei, the merchant whom the king had met while he was hostage in the nearby State of Zhao, prior to ascending the throne.

In 247 BC, when YingZheng was only 13 years old, his father died and he became King of Qin. Since he was too young to handle the affairs of State, Lu Buwei served as his regent and also the Prime Minister. Together with YingZheng's mother, the Queen, they administered the State of Qin. At the age of 22, YingZheng took over the reins of the government himself.

The first decision that he made was to put down a rebellion led by LaoAi, a servant who had become intimate with the Queen. The following year the young king removed his regent-Lu Buwei and exiled him to Sichuan, where he later committed suicide. Having all of his own civil affairs in order, the king began the task of conquering the six other states that existed at that time in ancient China, the states of Qi, Chu, Yan, Han, Zhao and Wei. In 221 BC, the King, at the age of 39, achieved his final victory and proclaimed the Qin Empire, declaring himself to be QinShiHuangDi, the first emperor. His territory extended from the sea in the south and east, LinTao in the west and Mount Yin and the area of LiaoDong in the north.

In order to consolidate his rule, Emperor Qin instituted a series of new policies. Probably his greatest contribution to the practice of government in China was the establishment of the centralized State and the abolition of the feudal system. He divided the country into 36 prefectures that were further broken down into counties, townships, Tings and Lis. He appointed twelve ministers who helped him make decisions of State affairs. By appointing the ministers directly, Emperor Qin had all the powers of the State in his hands.

A view of the Great Wall

Qinshihuang - the first emperor of China and the founder of the Qin Dynasty

To further unify the country, Emperor Qin standardized the system of weights and measures. He made Small Seal Script standard form of handwriting. And he ordered that the width of carriage axles be exactly six feet. These measures helped to centralize politics, economy, military

affairs and culture. To protect his policies, Emperor Qin ordered the destruction of many ancient records and Confucian writings. He had large numbers of Confucian scholars murdered.

Emperor Qin read reports from all parts of the country in order to be aware of problems anywhere in his domain. He had the reports weighed (Writings were inscribed on bamboo or wood at that time) and would not rest until he had read a certain weight of reports.

To ensure the security of his empire, he had a road network built over which he toured the furthest corners of his domain. Everywhere he went he had stone memorial tablets erected with inscriptions extolling his virtues and the laws of the State of Qin. To keep out invaders he ordered General MengTian to rebuild and connect the defensive walls of the states he had overcome into the Great Wall of China. It was accomplished by a huge labor force. He sent part of his army to guard five mountains in southern China and had a canal called the Lin Canal constructed.

QinShihuang undertook a vast construction program within the Empire. He expanded the size of his tomb and had large numbers of palaces built.

Drawing of the Qin Imperial Palace at Capital XianYang

The Apang Palace at his capital XianYang was built with "terraces that could seat ten thousand". SiMaqian's (145BC-86BC) *ShiJi* (Records of Historians) records: "Three hundred palaces were built within the Pass, and east of it more than four hundred. A large labor force was drafted to build Apang Palace and the emperor's tomb." Two million people or ten percent of the population of the State of Qin were used in the construction. The loss of this amount of farm labor damaged the economic development of the empire.

QinShihuang was convinced that he could find the elixir of life and expended great amounts of resources in an unsuccessful attempt to discover it, especially after 219 BC. He was told that "in the middle of the sea, there are three supernatural mountains called PengLai, FongZhang and Ying Zhou. Immortals live there". He was further told to go there with several thousand young boys and girls to find the Immortals. Despite all his attempts at immortality, he died at the relatively young age of 50.

QinShihuang was obsessed with a fear of death. No ministers dared to mention the word "death" to him, even though he was seriously sick on his last inspection tour through the Empire. As he became worse, he nominated his eldest son FuSu, a very able politician, to succeed to his throne. The letter confirming the domination was intrusted to ZhaoGao, the keeper of Chariots, to deliver to FuSu. The emperor hoped that this letter would cause FuSu to return to the capital XianYang to hold the funeral immediately after his death. ZhaoGao did not send the letter, however.

When Emperor Qin died away from the capital, ZhaoGao and Prime Minister LiSi did not announce his death. They hoped to appoint another of Qin's son, HuHai, whom Zhao Gao had taught to write and could easily influence, before it was known that Qin was dead. They destroyed the Imperial letter and forged another appointing HuHai as Crown Prince, while FuSu and commander-in chief MengTian were ordered to commit suicide.

While waiting for news of suicide, the plotters delayed the news of Qin's death and the return of his body to the capital. However, his body began to decompose and smell. They covered it up by having a chariot of fish follow the emperor's. Once the suicides were confirmed, they released the death notice. Emperor Qin's body was buried in the mausoleum in September 210 BC.

HuHai became the Second Emperor that year. He was not an able politician and was unable to make decisions. ZhaoGao gradually took over the powers of the state. HuHai also lived an even more luxurious life than his father. A peasant rebellion put an end to the Qin dynasty just fifteen years after it had begun. Despite its short duration, it had great influence and laid the foundation for the success of future dynasties.

Emperor Qin's mausoleum is situated at the northern foot of Mount Li, some 35 kilometers east of Xi'an city. Mount Li stands 1,256 meters high with trees evergreen all year around. The ShuiJingZhu (The Water Classic) records: "The southern side of Mount Li is famous for gold and the northern side for jade." The main reason why the emperor selected this site is its good FengShui.

FengShui is the art of positioning manmade structures in harmony with the vital cosmic energy coursing through the earth. It is quite essential for Chinese in its concern for harmony and proportion, and for balancing man, nature and spirit.

Traditional cosmology describes how the invisible energy currents, or Dragon Veins, run from the sky down into mountain peaks and then along the earth, blending heavenly and earthly energies. Natural topography the forms of hills, the direction of streams is believed to modify the natural energies, creating auspicious and inauspicious sites.

The ideal site faces south, with rising land to the east and softly undulating hills to the west. It has a stream in front and mountains in the back and is open to breezes in front. It is dry and has no white ants. Often these sites are used for graves: ancestors must be appeased with the best of everything.

According to FengShui theory, Emperor Qin finally decided to construct his mausoleum with evergreen Mount Li to the south and the Wei River to the north. A second reason was that this site was already the burial area of the Qin Kings. After the capital of the State of Qin moved from western to eastern China, the Kings of Qin were buried here as well. Ancient Chinese believed it was important to bury their kings near the capital. Once the capital was founded in XianYang, the zone between XianYang and Mount Li became the burial region for the Qin family. The tomb of Emperor Qin's father is only about 10 kilometers west of his.

The massive construction of Emperor Qin's mausoleum created a precedent for the emperors after him. Burial mounds that conceal tombs below them had appeared early in the late Spring and Autumn Period (770 BC--476 BC), but none was as huge as Emperor QinShihuang's mausoleum. The custom of building a huge mausoleum started with Emperor Qin and the emperors in the later dynasties, the Han, the Tang and others followed his example.

Emperor Qin's mausoleum was originally named LiShan Garden. People in China did not worship their Gods and ancestors at the graves and tombs before Emperor Qin. This tradition began with this emperor, who had his resting hall built alongside the mausoleum. LiYi, the administrative office of the tomb, was set up in the vicinity of the mausoleum, also a first in Chinese history.

Construction on the mausoleum started soon after QinShihuang became King of Qin. It was managed directly by the ministers of Qin Empire, but ShaoFu was the man most in charge. Construction took 38 years from 247 BC to 208 BC and was divided into three stages. The first phase, from 247 BC to 230 BC consisted of small-scale construction. During the second stage from 230 BC to 221 BC, the State of Qin defeated the other states and unified the country. Building was on a larger scale during this second phase but not as massive as the final phase because the State was involved in the wars. During the last phase, from 221 BC to 208 BC, construction peaked with as many as 720,000 conscripts.

The construction of Emperor Qin's Mausoleum lasted nearly 40 years. At one point it became difficult to dig in the earth and Minister LiSi sent a report to the Emperor: " It seems that we have reached the bottom of the earth and can not dig any more." Emperor ordered him to try again. It is apparent that the emperor took great care of his mausoleum and required that it be as large as possible.

Emperor Qin died in 210 BC while on the fifth tour of his empire. He devoted his whole life to search for the elixir of immortality. He never imagined that he would leave this world at the young age of 50. The tomb was not complete when his body was buried within it. According to a decree of the Second Emperor, those of his

The Qin Dynasty Terra-Cotta Army of

The burial mound of QinShihuang's mausoleum, situated 1.5 kilometers west of the Terra-cotta Museum

father's ladies who had no children were ordered to follow the emperor to the grave. Many of the tomb builders were also buried alive. In the *HanShu*(Book Of Han), the emperor's funeral was described as follows: " thousands of officials were killed and thousands of craftsmen were buried alive in order to keep the tomb secret." Construction was incompletely finished during the reign of the Second Emperor, due to the interference of a series of the peasant revolts.

Emperor Qin believed that life under the ground after death was a continuation of life on earth. Therefore he constructed a huge mausoleum for himself. At the same time he left his highly developed civilization to people today.

Awakened
Qin's Terra-Cotta Army

Emperor Qin's Mausoleum and the Satellite Pits and Tombs

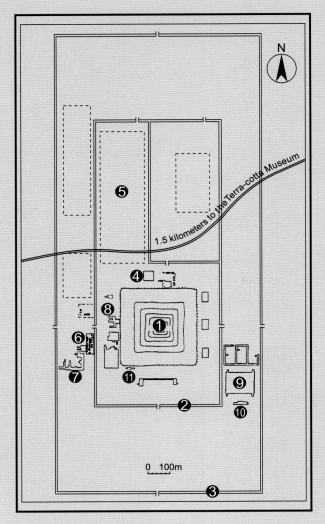

Location map showing Emperor Qin's Mausoleum and some discovered satellite pits and tombs

1.The burial mound of QinShihuang's mausoleum
2.Inner wall of burial mound
3.Outer wall of burial mound
4.The resting hall
5.The side hall
6.Pits of rare birds and animals
7.Stable Pits
8.Pit of two sets of bronze chariots and horses
9.Pit of stone armor and helmets
10.Pit of terra-cotta acrobats
11.Pit of terra-cotta civil officials

Emperor QinShihuang's mausoleum is huge and magnificent and can be seen from far away. The construction of the emperor's tomb is recorded in the *ShiJi*(Records of the historian) as follows: they dug through three streams and poured molten copper for the outer coffin, and the tomb was fitted with models of palaces, pavilions and officials, as well as fine vessels, precious stones and other rarities. Artisans were ordered to fix up crossbows so any thief breaking in would be shot. All the country's streams, the Yellow River and Yangtze were reproduced in quicksilver and by some mechanical means made to flow. The heavenly constellations were shown above and the regions of the earth below. The candles were made of whale oil to ensure their burning for eternity.

The description tells us that Emperor QinShihuang's mausoleum was actually an underground treasure house. The tomb was a subterranean palace with a protective outer wall 6,210 meters in perimeter on the ground level. Within this area was an inner wall that surrounded the burial mound, located in the southern half of the overall compound. Both of the walls had watch-towers and gates leading out in all four directions. The burial mound was 115 meters high 2,200 years ago. Due to the passage of time it is reduced to 76 meters today. With the emperor's tomb as the center, some 600 satellite pits and tombs have been found within the area of 56.25 square kilometers and more continue to be discovered.

The bronze music bell with gold-silver-inlaid patterns

The resting hall of the emperor is situated 5 meters north of the burial mound. It was once a large building above ground covering an area of 3,575 square meters, where there were all the necessities of daily life, as if the emperor were still alive. The side hall, a subsidiary building of the resting hall, is located north of the resting hall. Here the tomb owner could rest and relax.

Three sets of ruins, probably small palaces of some sort, have been discovered in the northwest corner between the inner wall and the outer wall. They were most likely ritual sites and living quarters for the tomb officials. This is revealed by some of the relics unearthed here such as a bronze music bell with a gold and silver inlaid inscription, a bronze Quan, the standard weighing apparatus, fragments of a bronze lamp with goose-shaped leg and some broken pieces of a porcelain bottle.

The half-round eaves tile which measures 48cm in height and 61cm in diameter is the largest ancient tile thus discovered from the ruin of the resting hall.

View of the ruin of the administrative office of the mausoleum

1 Pits of Rare Birds and Animals:

Thirty-one pits of rare animals and birds have been unearthed within the confines of the wall on the western side of the mausoleum. The animals and birds are accompanied by a few attendants. These finds indicate the Emperor's love for hunting.

2 Stable Pits:

Ninety-eight sets of stable pits were found at ShangJiaoCun, a village 350 meters east of the mausoleum. In front of the horses were placed some pottery jars, basins and lamps in these pits. The remains of millets and hay were still left in the basins. These pits were modeled after Qin's imperial stable system. They help to clarify the method of raising horses in the Qin imperial stables.

The pottery figures of a kneeling attendants excavated in the stable pit

The pottery jar

The pottery plate

The pottery basin

The pottery basin

· ·

3 Tombs of Emperor Qin's Children:

Archaeologists have found seventeen Qin tombs for Emperor QinShihuang's princes and princesses killed by the Second Emperor. They were placed on both sides of the stable pits, eight meters distant from them. Eight of these tombs have been unearthed. They are in the 甲-shape with sloping roadways leading to the tombs. In the tombs approximately two hundred historical relics made of different materials such as gold, silver, bronze, iron, pottery, jade, shellfish, bone have been discovered. Lacquer ware and fragmented silk has also been found.

The seal

The bronze mirror

4 Mass Graves:

In present day ZhaoBeiHuCun, a village southwest of the mausoleum, "mass graves" have been discovered, covering an area of 8,100 square meters. 42 of them have been unearthed and over a hundred human skeletons were found. The skeletons were tossed together in simple graves. In one grave the skeletons are piled on one another, some appearing to be struggling, suggesting that they were buried alive. Based on the evidence of inscriptions on tile fragments, with names and birth--places, it is presumed that these were laborers killed during or after the construction work.

Full view of the excavation site of the builders' tombs

Full view of the excavation site of the builders' tombs

The tile fragments with inscriptions of the names and birth places of the death, the earliest epitaphs which have been unearthed so far

Full view of the excavation site of the Bronze Chariots and Horses

The restored No.1 Chariot

The restored No.2 Chariot

5 Pit of Two Sets of Bronze Chariots and Horses:

In December 1980, archaeologists discovered a large pit holding two sets of painted bronze chariots and horses, 20 meters west of the Emperor Qin's tomb mound. The pit is about 7.8 meters beneath the present ground level. The bronze chariots and horses were originally placed in a big wooden coffin. Over time the wood has rotted and the earthen layers has collapsed. The chariots and horses were found in thousands of pieces. Fortunately, the pit was not robbed. The pieces were scattered on the ground. After eight years of painstaking restoration, two complete sets of bronze chariots and horses are on display in the museum.

Investigation reveals that the chariots were the deluxe sedans to be used by the emperor when he went on inspection tours in his after life. They were modeled after the real chariot, horse and driver, but were half size. Bronze was used for making chariots, horses and charioteers with large amounts of gold and silver

used for ornamentation. The chariots and horses were cast in perfect proportion. They were painted to look even more magnificent and noble. Archaeologists named them the "High Chariot" and the "Comfortable Chariot". Each chariot had a single shaft, two wheels and is drawn by four horses. They are the biggest and most realistic bronze chariots and horses that have been unearthed so far.

High Chariot: The chariot with the horses in front, is 2.57 meters long and weights 1,061 kilos. It is also called a "Battle Carriage" or an "Inspection Carriage". On the outer side of the left protecting board is a quiver in which 12 bronze arrows are laid. On the inner side of the right protecting board there is a bronze shield inserted in a set of silver shield-holders. Both sides of the shield are colorfully painted by cloud-like patterns. This shield is the most complete shield ever discovered from the Qin Dynasty.

To restore No.1 Chariot

The charioteer stands on the chariot looking ahead with a prudent and humble facial expression. He wears headgear and his square-toed shoes curve slightly towards the ankles. He is armed with a long sword and decorated with a jade ring at the waist. Both of his arms are extending forward. The thumb is apart from the forefinger, while his other fingers hold the bridle reins. The fingers are thin and long. The fingernails are round and full. His hands look amazingly real.

Comfortable Chariot: The Comfortable Chariot and its horses is 3.17 meters long and weighs 1,241 kilos. The carriage is divided into a front chamber and a back chamber. The charioteer sits in the front chamber driving the chariot. He has the same costume as the driver of the High Chariot but he looks more humble. The back chamber is quite spacious, 0.78 meters wide and 0.88 meters long. The window panels of the back chamber are cast into shallow diamond-flower holes, which are neatly aligned into rhombic patterns. The holes are used for ventilation. Therefore the Comfortable Chariot is also called "Air-conditioned Chariot" of 2,200 years ago. The roof of the carriage is a turtle-shell canopy. The canopy is 1.78 meters long, 1.29 meters wide.

Workmanship: The thinness of bronze walls is one of the most significant characteristics of the bronze chariots. The thickest position of the canopies is 4mm while the thinnest position is only 1.5mm. The canopy of the Comfortable Chariot covers an area of 2.3 square meters. Creating such a canopy would not be an easy job even today.

Restoration of the canopy of No.1 Chariot

Restoration of the canopy of No.1 Chariot

The restored canopy of No.1 Chariot

Charioteer of No.2 Chariot

Charioteer of No.1 Chariot

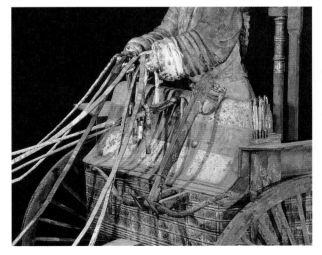

Charioteer of No.1 Chariot with reins in hands

Charioteer of No.2 Chariot with reins in hands

Back view of the Charioteer of No.1 Chariot

Jade ring at the waist for decoration

Back view of the horses

The arrow quiver in the carriage of No.1 Chariot

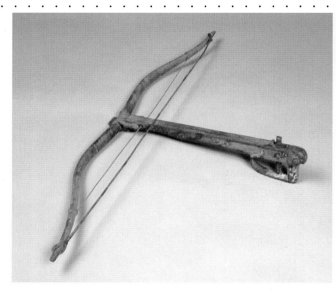

The crossbow in No.1 Chariot

Color painting on the front surface of the shield

Color painting on the inside surface of the shield

Driving and Harnessing Mechanism: Both High Chariot and Comfortable Chariot are of the single-shaft type. The horses pull the yokes. The yokes are linked with the balance block. The balance block pulls the shaft and the shaft pulls the wagon. Each chariot has four horses, two in front of the carriage and one on each side of those horses. To keep the four horses pulling steadily and the chariots walking smoothly, each set of horses has a bronze belly-drive suspended at the outer ribs of the two central horses. On the end of the belly-drive there are four sharp cones protruding towards the side horses. If the side horses walk in, the cones would stab them, causing pain. If the side horses walk out, the rope round the side horses would be stretched tight.

The teeth engraved in the mouths of the horses indicate that the horses are all six years old, the best age for draught. The coarse-fiber tassel on the head of each right side horse is a symbol of the social position and authority of the passenger.

Belly-drive between the central-horse and the side-horse

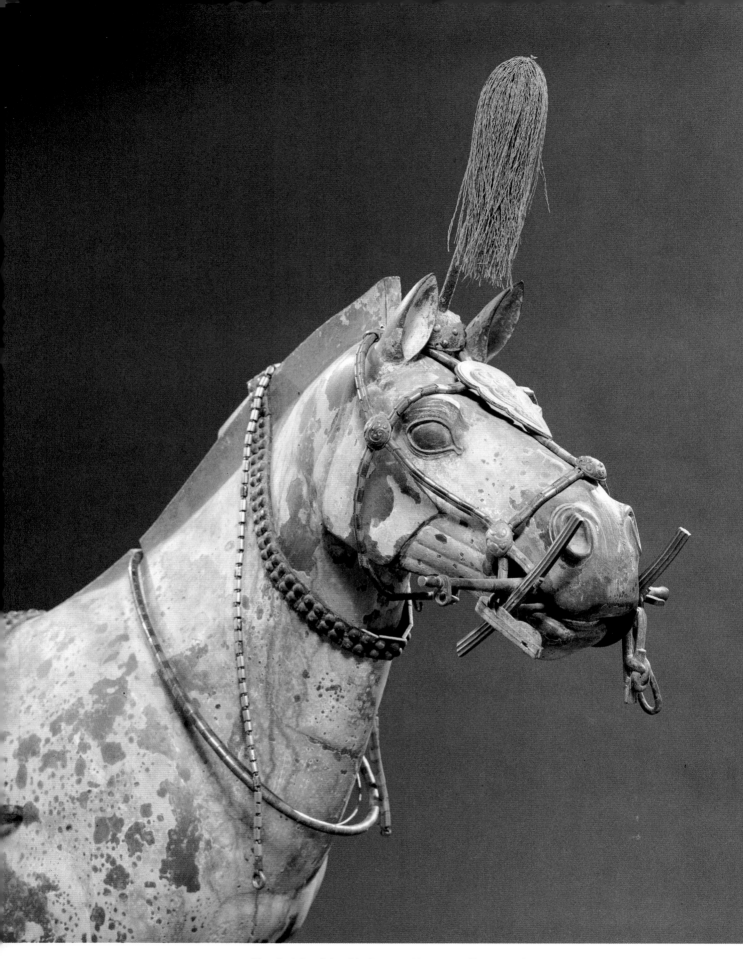

Head of the right side-horse with coarse-fiber tassel

Coloring of the Chariots: Both chariots were originally painted with bright colors ranging from vermilion, pink, green, blue to white but the basic color was white. The Chinese of that time believed in the "Yin-Yang" theory. Outer space and earth were divided into five directions represented by five colors: red, black, yellow, blue and white. The colors represented south, north, the center, east and west respectively. The bronze chariots used white to indicate the west direction. This suggests that four other sets of bronze chariots and horses will be discovered in the future, painted with the colors of the other directions.

There are more than ten color patterns on the chariots depicting dragons, phoenixes, diamonds, clouds and geometric designs. The layer of color has protected the bronze, delaying oxidation, although the Qin people did not realize it at the time.

Color patterns on the inner side of the front board of No.1 Chariot

Color patterns on the cabin-walls of No.2 Chariot

The Newly Unearthed Pit--Stone Armor and Helmets:

6 In 1998 archaeologists discovered a large burial pit containing stone armor and stone helmets, some 200 meters southeast of the emperor's mausoleum. The pit is rectangular in shape, covering an area of 13,600 square meters. It is the largest burial pit that has been unearthed so far within the confines of the inner and outer walls. Nearly 120 stone armor suits and 90 stone helmets have been unearthed. These objects were scattered in disarray on the bottom of the pit. Several pillars supported a wooden ceiling coated by layers of straw. Different sections of the pit were separated by rammed earth.

View of excavation site of the pit of the stone armor and helmets

The armor and helmet were made from numerous stone flakes. The stone material was fine-grained limestone in a dark gray color. The stone they made from is easy to break, with poor toughness and heavy weight. The main flakes are rectangular, square, trapezoid and round in shape, some are in special shape. There are some round and square tiny holes on the stone flakes for stringing with flat copper wires. The edge of non-overlapped flakes is artistically decorated by a groove. The overlapped corners are made round with the aim of linking, expanding and contracting flakes. Judging from the features, archaeologists divide the armor suits into three categories:

Small stone flakes: Two pieces of this kind armor have been unearthed. The stone pieces are small and thin but exquisitely made, just like fish scales. Both armor suits are composed of over 800 stone flakes.

Medium stone flakes: This kind takes up over 80% of the stone armors that have been discovered. Most of the stone flakes are in rectangular or square shape with tiny holes for linking or for decoration.

Large stone flakes: Only one piece of this kind has been unearthed. It is 1.8 meters in length with armor flakes measuring 14×7cm. From its shape and structure, it's believed to be used for the battle steed. Historical book tells that the horse armor didn't appear until the end of the Eastern Han Dynasty, but this armor pushed the origin of horse-armor-making at least 400 years earlier.

At the present time, only one set of stone armor and one stone helmet have been restored. The armor weighs about 18 kilograms and the helmet weighs about 3.1 kilograms with 74 flakes linked together.

The objects were made the same size as real armor coats and helmets. According to archaeologists, they were not for practical use like the iron or leather armor of that era. These might have been specially made as funeral objects for Emperor QinShihuang.

To restore the stone armor

The restored stone armor suit

The restored stone helmet

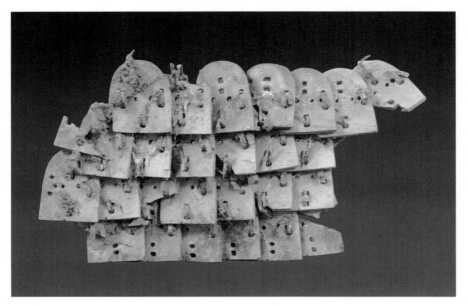

Restored piece of the stone armor suit

7 The Newly Unearthed Pit--Terra-cotta Acrobats and a Bronze Tripod:

In addition to the chamber of armor, archaeologists have found another pit 40 meters south of the stone armor and helmets pit. The trial excavation on an area of only 9 square meters of the pit in rectangular shape unearthed 12 pottery figurines and "No.1 bronze Ding Tripod" of the Qin Dynasty on the top layer of the same pit.

Similar to real people in size, the figurines were only clothed in a short skirt in a shape similar to those of woman's miniskirt today. Some appear tall and strong while some others short and slim. Exquisitely made, the figures vary in posture. One has his hand raised and another holds a piece of his skirt. Compared with the serious expressions on the terra-cotta warriors, these figures were more active and expressive.

According to an analysis of the restored figures, archaeologists said, different from the terra-cotta warriors, these pottery figures might be the acrobats who served in the Emperor Qin's imperial palace, portraying the splendid acrobatic art of the Qin Dynasty.

The restored pottery acrobats

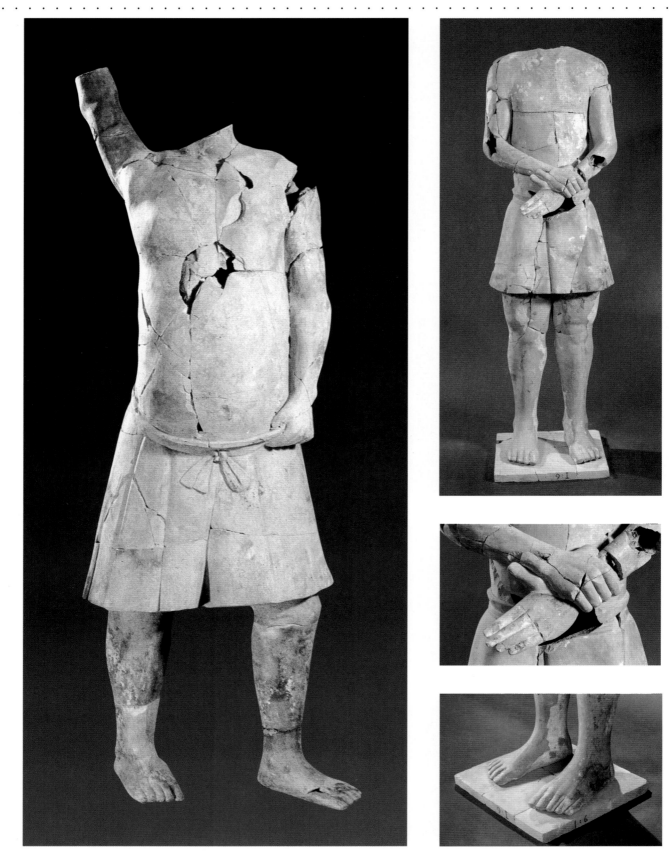

The restored pottery acrobats

The bronze tripod unearthed on the top of the 12 acrobats is the biggest and heaviest one which has been found so far from the Emperor Qin's mausoleum. It is 59.5 centimeters in length, 64 centimeters in diameter and 212 kilograms weight.

The tripod was originally a cooking utensil for boiling meat. With the consolidation of the system of hierarchical rites and music, it also became a symbol of stratum. This bronze tripod was delicately shaped with rich, fluid and beautiful patterns. Again, due to the lack of historical records, experts estimated that it might be a piece of sacrificial offering of that era.

The bronze Tripod unearthed on the top layer of the acrobats

The leg of the bronze tripod

The newly unearthed pottery
civil official

8 The Newly Unearthed Pit--Civil Officials:

In October 2,000, another new burial pit located southwest of the emperor's tomb mound was discovered.

Only a few pottery figures unearthed from the pit have been restored. The figures have colorful paint remained on the faces. The facial expression is gentle and humble. They dress in similar costume as the pottery warriors in the burial army pits located 1.5 kilometers east away. The hands have no weapons, but cross at the waist and covered by long, loose sleeves. Each of them wears a knife and a knife-sharpener at the waist. The knife was used as the present eraser for peeling wrong notes inscribed on wood or bamboo, because paper had not been invented during the Qin period. The unique knife and knife-sharpener are the first of their kind so far unearthed from the emperor's mausoleum.

It is estimated that these pottery figures might be the sub mid-ranking civil officials who served in the Central Government of Qin Empire.

Knife and knife-sharpener on the waist of the civil official

Head of the pottery civil official

A close-up of the bronze crane's head

The bronze crane

A close-up of the bronze crane's feather

9 The Newly Unearthed Pit-- Bronze Birds:

Early in July 2000, local farmers had discovered some pottery fragments when they built the tombs northwest of the Terra-cotta Army Museum and 3 kilometers northeast away from the emperor's tomb. By November 2002, a piece of exciting news was released there: a pit of Qin Dynasty's bronze birds was first found in the area of QinShihuang's mausoleum.

The pit is of F-shape about 925 square meters. It is a subterranean pit consists of one sloping roadway, two corridors in south and north's axis and one in east and west's axis. The trial excavation analysis the pit's construction as the followings: The earth-rammed platform erected on both sides of the corridor, is paved with square wooden boards on which the bronze birds were placed. The archaeologists unearthed 13 bronze birds and 5 pieces of pedestal. Excavations showed that these bronze birds used to stand on the pedestals and scattered regularly on the platform. But much was damaged and had their

View of the excavation site of the pit of the bronze birds

The bronze goose

spread slightly. The other one next to it has a S-shaped neck, it seems he is concentrating on catching fish.

Standing on the cloud-patterned pedestals is perhaps the most interesting characteristic of these bronze birds. The Qin artists hoped the pedestals could help the birds stand steadily. Secondly, the birds seemed to fly among the clouds. Ancient Chinese regarded the crane as longevity. So some archaeologists think that Emperor Qin built this pit specially for showing his attempts at immortality.

places changed by burial underneath the ground for thousands of years, fires and the pressure of the burial chambers' roofs, etc.

The bronze birds are different in sizes, but similar to real birds. The taller one is about 60 to 70cm, and the shorter one is 48cm. The recent unearthed bronze birds are known as the cranes and geese. They are exquisitely made and vary in posture. One has a straight neck with its wings

The bronze swan

The construction of QinShihuang's mausoleum required considerable resources and manpower at that time. In present day, continuous excavations are going on. Archaeologists are sure that more and more treasures will be brought to light in future.

It was in March 1974, when local farmers were drilling a well in search of water, that large pottery fragments were discovered 1.5 kilometers east of Emperor Qin's Mausoleum. This finds subsequently led to the revelation of one pit of the First Emperor's buried army 2,200 years ago. Since then continual archaeological work on excavation discovered another two pits successively. It has been revealed that three underground pits totally cover an area of 22,000 square meters, housing an estimated 8,000 life-size pottery warriors and horses.

The three pits were built in similar basic construction. They are five to seven meters beneath the present ground level with the terra-cotta figures placed in corridors. The corridors, divided by earth-rammed partition walls, are paved with pottery bricks on which the figures were placed. The earth walls sustained wood roof that was composed of huge and strong rafters, the roof was covered by layers of fiber mats, fine soil and tilled earth. All these were constructed to totally conceal the army.

The three pits vary in size and shape. Pit 1 is the largest one in rectangular shape, housing the main force of the army; Pit 2 is located some 20 meters north of Pit 1, which is a complex battle formation formed by charioteers, archers, cavalrymen and infantrymen. It is specially used for supporting the main force; Pit 3 located 25 meters to the north of Pit 1 and to the west of Pit 2, was evidently the headquarter. The total three pits are located to the east of Emperor's Mausoleum, determining that the army was facing east, with its back to the tomb, serving as guardians to protect the entrance of the Emperor's burial.

The first discovery at the east end of Pit 1 in 1974

Pit No. 1:

Pit 1, the largest pit, is in a rectangular shape. It measures 230 meters long from east to west, 62 meters wide from north to south and 5 meters deep, covering an area of 14,260 square meters. Five sloping roadways into the pits were constructed on eastern and western sides of pits to permit access.

The terra-cotta warriors and horses are arrayed in a practical battle formation. At the eastern end of the pit there are three rows of vanguards, 68 in each, totaling 204 soldiers who were originally equipped with genuine bows and crossbows. Immediately behind the vanguards is the main body of the battle formation: 30 chariots, each of which was drawn by four horses, armored and unarmored soldiers held weapons originally, such as spears, halberds etc. Around the outer edge, there is one row of soldiers with crossbows facing south, north and west respectively as the flanks to guard the sides and rear of the army. According to the density of each trial trench that has been excavated, it's assumed that more than 6,000 pottery warriors and horses will be unearthed from Pit 1, most of which are infantrymen.

General view of Pit 1 with restored figures replaced in their original position. Excavation work is still continuing

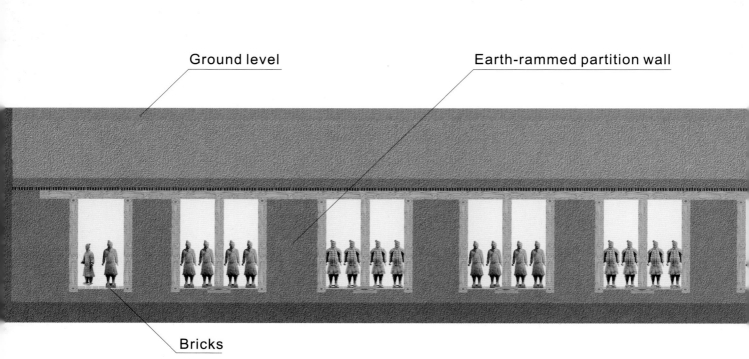

Ground level   Earth-rammed partition wall

Bricks

Drawing of a cross-section of Pit 1 showing the timber framework that was constructed over the corridors housing the terra-cotta figures

N

⌐⌐ Sloping roadway   ≡∷∷ Excavated and un-excavated earth-rammed partition wall   🚩 Chariot drawn by four horses   ○ Un-armored warrior   ◑ Armored warrior

Diagram of Pit 1 showing the estimated layout of the 6,000 pottery figures and horses

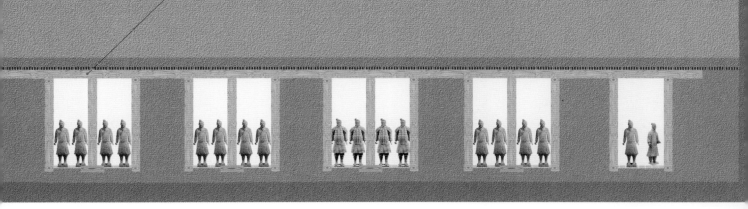

Layers of timber, fiber matting, earth fill and tilled earth

0   2m

Side view of Pit 1

Section of the battle array in Pit 1

The remnants of a chariot in Pit 1

Side view of vanguards in Pit 1

Pit No. 2:

Located 20 meters to the north of Pit 1 at the eastern end, Pit 2 is in "L" shape with a protruding rectangular area at the northeast corner. This pit was discovered in 1976, covering an area of 6,000 square meters. Different from Pit 1, over 1,300 pottery figures in Pit 2 were placed in four specialized military forces:

The protruding northeast area houses 332 archers in all, 160 kneeling archers were arrayed into four columns with 172 standing archers surrounding. All these archers, whatever kneeling or standing soldiers, face eastward.

The south area is composed of war chariots. Total 64 chariots were arrayed in 8 columns, also facing east, eight chariots with their chariot horses in each column. Originally made of wood, the chariots were completely deteriorated when unearthed. Each chariot in this group was accompanied with a charioteer, who was flanked by two attendant soldiers carrying long weapons.

The middle area consists of war chariots in the front, immediately followed by infantrymen and the cavalry at the rear.

The north area has only cavalry. There are totally 108 cavalrymen. Each of the cavalrymen stands in front of his saddled war-horse, holding the reins in right hand and a bow in left hand.

The four arrays seemed to exist independently, but could be assembled immediately to constitute a complete battle formation during the war times. This reflected the unique military strategy of the Qin army--army array within army array.

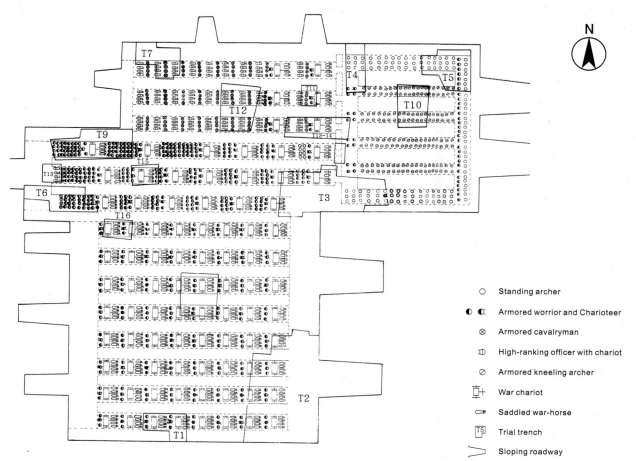

○	Standing archer
◑ ◖	Armored worrior and Charioteer
⊗	Armored cavalryman
Ⅹⅅ	High-ranking officer with chariot
⊘	Armored kneeling archer
🛒	War chariot
⊐	Saddled war-horse
T5	Trial trench
⟍	Sloping roadway

Diagram of Pit No.2 showing layout of pottery figures and chariots

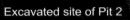
Excavated site of Pit 2

Excavated site of the chariots in Pit 2

Excavated site of the kneeling archers in Pit 2

The remnants of wood used to support the roof in Pit 2

Pit No. 3:

It is the smallest of the three pits and was discovered in 1976. Only 68 pottery figures and one chariot drawn by four horses were unearthed in the pit. It is of U-shape about 520 square meters. Pit 3 is now known as the command center of the entire army, because the following reasons:

Its position in the far northwest corner of the overall plan ensured that it was well protected by the armies of the two larger pits.

At the eastern end of the pit, there is a sloping road serviced as the entrance, then followed by an ornate canopied chariot with four armored soldiers. The chariot with canopy was colorful painted, representing higher rank.

In the north and south side chambers, 64 fully armored figures were found. Unlike the soldiers in Pit 1 and Pit 2, these figures were arrayed face-to-face with their backs to the wall, suggest that they were the guards. Even the weapons held by these guards are different from those in another two pits. One particular weapon named Shu, which had no blades, only unearthed from Pit 3, it was believed to be used by the guards of honor.

In north chamber, a piece of broken deer horn and some remains of animal bones were found at one time. They were used by generals as ritual objects for those religious practices, praying for the protection from the Gods before each battle.

Once the Terra-cotta warriors and horses were all arrayed inside the corridors, the entrances were closed. It meant a sealed united army was formed to guard Emperor Qin's underground palace.

車馬房
STABLE

北廂房
THE NORTHERN
CHAMBER

陳南遺跡
THE HISTORICAL REMAINS
OF THE SIDEWALK

戰車遺跡
THE HISTORICAL REMAINS
OF THE WAR CHARIOT

A full view of Pit 3

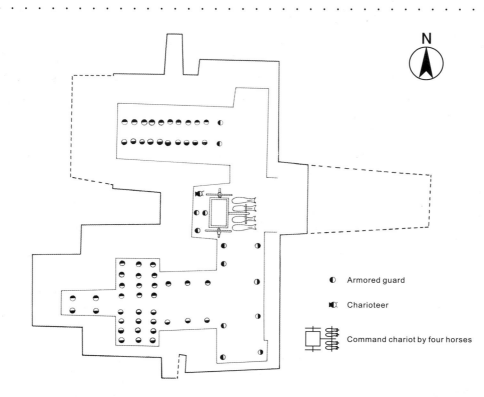

N

Armored guard

Charioteer

Command chariot by four horses

Diagram of Pit 3 showing layout of pottery figures and the single chariot of the commander

Restored chariot section of Pit 3

estored south section of Pit 3

Restored pottery figures in the south section of Pit 3

Excavated north site of Pit 3

The Terra-cotta Figures' Construction and Its Craftsmanship

In China the pottery figures could be dated back long time ago. But the pottery figures before the Qin Dynasty (221BC-206 BC) were roughly made in small size and the temperature for baking in the kiln was low, too. The Qin terra-cotta warriors and horses were big in life-size and exquisitely made with high technology. The hardness of their bodies indicates that they might be fired at a temperature between 950 and 1,050 degrees centigrade.

All of the soldiers and horses were made using local clay. The weight of the terra-cotta warriors varies from 110 to 300 kilos. Their average height is 1.8 meters. How were these large and heavy statues made 2,200 years ago? Investigations into the construction of the figures have shown that the same method was used throughout the entire production. In general,the bodies, heads and arms of the human figures are hollow and legs solid. The legs of the horses are also solid pottery, and these support a hollow body and head. Clearly such large figures could not have been produced from single mold and it seemed they were

constructed from a number of separately molded or modeled segments that were luted together before firing.

The construction of the human figures required a number of steps. The clay was sifted and washed to ensure an even texture and color and was combined with ground quartz. After repeated kneading, the wet clay would achieve the right degree of firmness. The feet and the pedestal on which they stood were hand made or molded with the legs. The torso was either sculpted from strips of clay or cast prior to the attachment of the arms. All the joints would have been sealed and strengthened with clay coils. The final step was the creation of the head. The heads of the human figures were made in two-piece molds that were joined together. Ears, noses and hair were hand made independently and then added on. In order to create an individualized appearance for each of the figures, such facial features as the mouth, moustache and beard and hairstyles were sculpted by probably a sharp bamboo. No two figures unearthed so far have the same features or expression. Some experts think that real soldiers served as models when terra-cotta warriors were made. Besides different faces, features as the armor plates with fixings, belt hooks, shoe ties and costume details were precisely sculpted. After each statue was made, the craftsmen were ordered to inscribe or print their names on the backs of robes, legs or armor. The names of over 80 craftsmen have been so far discovered. These seemed to be 2000-year-ago quality control.

The same principles of construction were employed in the making of the horses. The legs of the horses are all solid pottery to ensure that they would be strong. The head, body and tail were all molded or modeled separately and then fixed to the legs. The various details of the eyes, nostrils and mouth of the horses were sculpted the same way as the human figures. Both the chariot and cavalry horses have a square cut mane, a neatly manicured two-pronged forelock and alert ears. The cavalry horse has a long, plaited and pendant tail and the chariot horse a shorter tied tail so as to keep it free of the harness and chariot shaft.

The most visible difference between the types is the molded detail of the saddle and girth on the cavalry horse.

After the terra-cotta warriors and horses were made, they were put into the kilns to be fires. The heads of the human figures were fired separately from the body, so the necks were left like holes. Both horse types have round holes in each side of the body, too. These holes could permit the gases and vapors that would have built up in the kiln to escape, prevent the figures from deforming or exploding.

Sketch Model **of the** Construction **of the** Pottery Human Figure

Sketch Model **of the** Construction **of the** Pottery Horse

One piece of the head molds with hand's trace left by craftsman 2,200 years ago

trips of clay for coiling the torso of the pottery human figure

The individualized facial characteristics of the terra-cotta warriors

Hairstyles of the terra-cotta warriors

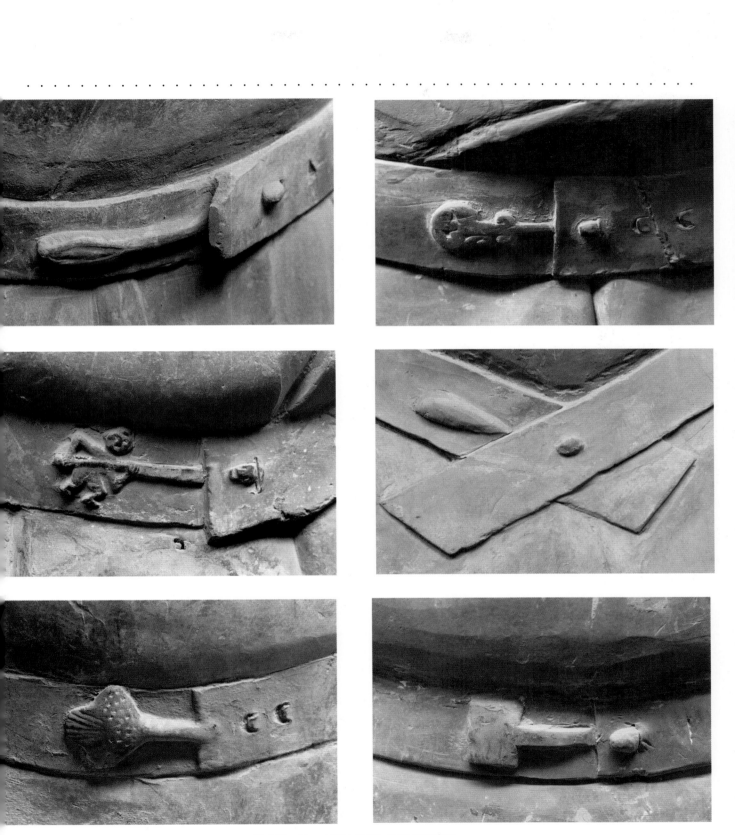

Belt Buckles of the terra-cotta warriors

Beards and mustaches of the terra-cotta warriors

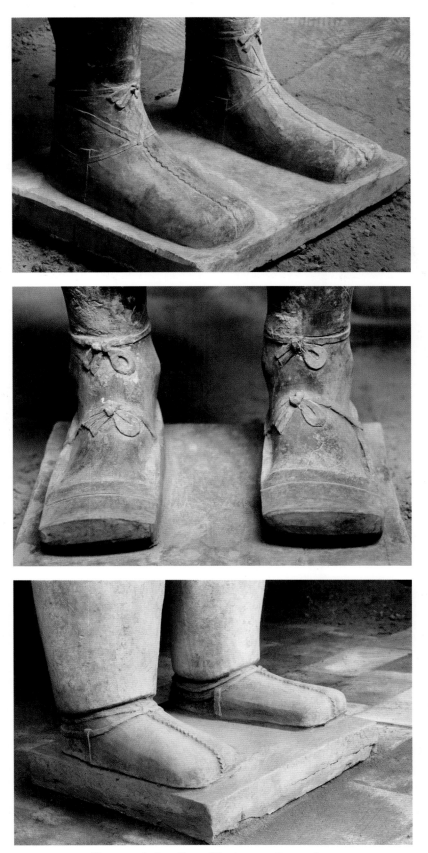

Shoes and shoe ties of the terra-cotta warriors

Inscriptions of the names of craftsmen on the terra-cotta warriors

The head of the pottery horse

Full view of a chariot horse with holes for permitting the gases and vapors in the kiln to escape

The tied tail of the chariot horse

The plaited pendant tail of the cavalry horse

The saddle and girth on the cavalry horse

The Colorful Uniform of Qin Terra-cotta Figures

The range of terra-cotta figure types represented in QinShihuang's army is more extensive. There are about seven main categories as follows: high-ranking officer, officer, armored and unarmored soldier, charioteer, cavalryman, kneeling archer and standing archer. The officer class is identified by their greater size and more ornate armor including headgear and small tabs or sashes which may be emblems of rank. The cavalryman is immediately identifiable by the tight fitting helmet tied under the chin, together with tight fitting armor to the waist and flared robe to facilitate riding. The charioteer is identifiable by the fully armored sleeves and the position of the hands, held firmly out in front as if to hold the reins.

Archaeologists have determined that originally the figures were completed with painted details, but ravages of floods, fire and time have erased original paint from statues. However, guided by flakes of paint remained on the figures, an approximation of the figures' original appearances can be modified as follows. Two new points can be

known from them: Qin army had no standardized colors for uniform and various colors can not help distinguish different ranks. It means that warriors of different ranks sometimes wore the same color clothing homely made.

The unearthed color-painted heads of the terra-cotta warriors

High Ranking Officer, Possibly a General
Height 197 cm,
From Pit 2, Qin Terra-cotta Museum

The officer's gesture and size give him a majestic presence. He is wearing double-layered robes covered by shoulder plates. Evidence suggests that his outer robe were painted dark purple and the robe beneath vermilion. His trousers were in green and his square-toed shoes in black. The headgear he is wearing was painted brown. The colorful fish-scaled armor protected the chest, back and shoulders. The armor was usually painted brown and dotted with vermilion thread for linking the pieces.

The collar, chest, shoulders and edges of the armor were decorated with colorful patterns. There are eight knots made of ribbon to decorate the armor, three knots on the front plate, three on the back and one knot each on the shoulder. His carefully groomed mustache and sideburns convey a sense of authority, solemnity and dignity.

High ranking officer

Painted reconstruction of high ranking officer

Officer
From Pit 2, Qin Terra-cotta Museum

The officer was wearing red trousers and a high-collar robe in green under an armor cape originally. The collar and cuff were decorated by white and red patterns. Both his flat hat and square-toed shoes should be in black. The figure wears chest armor, which is fastened by cross-straps on the back, over a flared battle robe. The ornate scarves around the neck possibly signify his commissioned rank.

From the position of the hands and arms, it's clear that this figure held weapons.

Front view of the officer

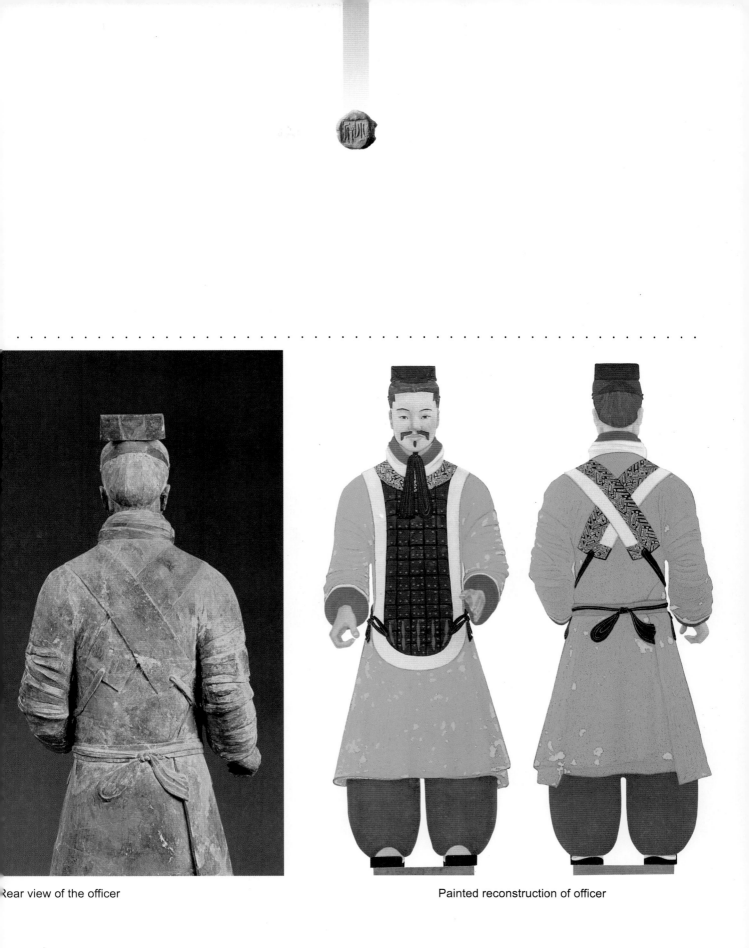

Rear view of the officer

Painted reconstruction of officer

The Armored and Un-armored Soldiers: A large quantity of soldiers has been discovered from the terra-cotta pits. Some of them wear armor, some don't. The colors of their uniform were much different when they painted. But the armors were all painted brown, without the colorful patterns on. The robes varied in colors as vermilion, green or blue, and the trousers green, white or pink.

Un-armored Soldier
From Pit 1 Qin Terra-cotta Museum

The figure wears knee-length robe without armor-plated uniform. Around the waist of the robe is a belt linked with a distinctive belt hook. The soldier also wears the short trousers and his shoes curve upward. The hair is tightly coiled into a neat bun on the right top of his head. The fact that he wears no armor allows for unrestricted movement.

Armored Officer
Height 182 cm,
From Pit 3 Qin Terra-cotta Museum

The figure wears a battle robe with full body armor including shoulder pieces. He also wears short trousers, curve-toed shoes. The right arm is raised and would evidently have held spear.

Un-armored soldier

Armored officer

Charioteer
From Pit 2 Qin Terra-cotta Museum

The figure was provided with a special uniform with extra armor to protect his arms, hands, neck and upper body. This was necessary because he needed to use both hands to hold the reins, and thus could not defend himself. His hands held firmly out in front to hold the reins.

The attendant soldiers, who flank the charioteer, wear long robes in different colors, one is in red, another in green. Both soldiers carry long weapons in one hand while grasping the chariot with the other.

Charioteer flanked by two soldiers

Painted reconstruction of the right and left flanking soldiers

Cavalryman

Height 180cm

From Pit 2 Qin Terra-cotta Museum

The cavalry was an important element of Emperor Qin's army, providing it with speed and agility. The figures of cavalrymen so far discovered were placed in Pit 2, together with their horses.

This figure wears the short dark brown tight-fitting armor, green narrow-sleeved knee-length robe originally. Beneath the belted waist the robe appears full with pleats and folds. The small tight-fitting cap fastened under the chin was originally painted a reddish brown, suggesting leather. The stitched leather shoes are represented in some details with lacing and ties. The figure holds the reins in one hand and a crossbow in the other.

The molded saddle on the horse's back with hand-finished carved probably represents a leather originally. A series of black circles symbolizing tacks are molded on the surface of the saddle, which were painted red, white, brown and blue. The saddle was held in place by a girth underneath the belly of horse.

Cavalryman with his horse

Kneeling Archer

Height 120cm

From Pit 2 Qin Terra-cotta Museum

The figures of kneeling archers were discovered from Pit 2. They own quite similar characteristics.

The figure wears green battle robe covered by armor together with shoulder pieces. The battle robe was distinguished by the series of pleats and folds as it rests over the legs. As with all of the terra-cotta figures, the archer was highly detailed, even showing the pebbled surface texture on the soles of his shoes. The hair was plaited on the back of the head and then coiled into a bun tied with vermilion ribbons.

He kneels on the right knee with the left knee raised. The right arm is held with the hand open, the left arm rests on the raised left knee and the hand extends across the chest. The pose of both hands evidences that this figure held one crossbow originally. The head is held firm and the eyes look directly ahead. The straight back emphasizes the impressions of concentration and discipline.

Rear view of part of the kneeling archer

Sole of archer's shoes

Painted reconstruction of the kneeling archer

kneeling archer

Standing Archer
Height 178 cm

From Pit 2 Qin Terra-cotta Museum

There is a large number of standing archers discovered in Pit 2. Their uniforms were colorful painted when made.

This figure was dressed in an unarmored red robe fastened around the waist with a belt, short green trousers, white shin guards and short boots. His hair was coiled into a neat bun on the right top of his head. The archer displays a posture: the feet stand apart with the right foot turned outwards and the left foot forward. His body is carefully tilted to the left with his pendant left arm and raised right arm in front of the chest as if to hold a crossbow.

Standing archer

The Terra-cotta Army is not only a huge subterranean military battle formation, but also an armory of the Qin Dynasty. Approximately tens of thousands of weapons have been unearthed from the partly excavated section of the pits. The weapons can be divided into three categories: Long weapons, short weapons and long range weapons, such as spear, halberd, Shu, Pi, sword, Wu hook and cross-bow etc. Especially Pi and Wu hook are the first of their kind so far unearthed.

In ancient Chinese records there is much about Pi Weapon, but no complete weapon has ever been unearthed. Pi weapon belongs to Long weapons. Its head is about 30 cm long and looks like a dagger. A 3-meter long shaft is attached to its head. Pi is such kind of sharp weapons used to bayonet.

Bronze Pi weapon

Wu hook belongs to short weapons. It looks like a crescent moon and there are blades on both edges. Its head is flat and easy to hook. Because it first appeared in the State of Wu, hence the name Wu hook.

Some 30 bronze Shu weapons were unearthed in Pit No. 3. Shu weapon in Qin Dynasty was used for ceremonial purposes and a symbol of authority. It is shaped in a cylinder with the head looks like a triangular cone. The warriors in the Pit No. 3 with holding Shu weapons strengthened majestic atmosphere of the headquarter.

Bronze Shu weapon

Wu hook

Swords had the highest rank among the weapons in ancient China and were carried by well-known or high-ranking people. About 17 swords have been discovered so far from the Terra-cotta pits. Besides the general, some officers have swords in their hands, too. The longest sword is about 94.4cm, and the shortest one is 81cm. The sword discovered intact from Pit No. 1 originally would have been kept in a wooden scabbard that has been rotted. Its blade is narrow and thin with a ridge along the center. According to analysis, the surface of the sword contains 0.6 to 2% chromium, with a thickness of 10 micron, which acted as a protective coating against corrosion during the long burial. The modern chrome-plating technology appeared in western countries in 1920s to 1930s, but it had emerged in China 2,200 years before. In style and appearance the sword resembles the classic Zhou sword which continued to be used in the succeeding Han Dynasty. Many bronze swords have additional ornament, generally in the form of turquoise, gold, silver or jade inlay, at the guard and in the top surface of the pommel.

Crossbows and arrowheads belong to long range weapons. The trigger mechanism for a crossbow is a type that, having been invented towards the end of the Zhou Dynasty, quickly found favor and was widely used in Qin Dynasty. The trigger is composed of four separately cast pieces and is very much more powerful than any of its contemporary weapons as it could, fire a bronze bolt a distance of 800 meters. The arrowheads, the largest number among the weapons unearthed, are triangular cones and extremely sharp.

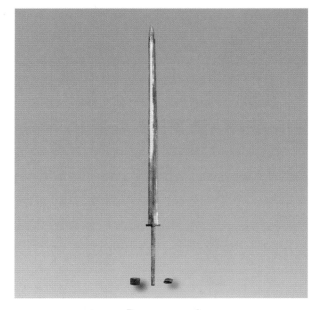

Bronze sword

Archaeologists have found almost every kind of weapons the Qin soldiers once used from the pits. The Qin weapons are not only in wide coverage, large number, but also advanced in technology. Ancient craftsmen had consciously regulated the proportions of the three main ingredients of bronze: copper, tin and lead, for casting weapons in different kinds. The bronze swords have a higher percentage of tin (21.3%) than in other bronze pieces from the excavation. This higher tin content resulted in an increased hardness comparable with tempered carbon steel. Advanced anti-rust technology of metal is another magnificent character of the Qin bronze weapons. Although the bronze swords had been buried for more than 2,000 years, they looked as shiny as new when they were unearthed, and could cut 19 pieces of paper. It was the chrome-plating technology 2,000 years ago protected the sharpness of the swords.

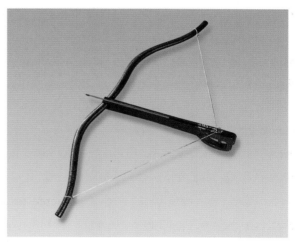

Crossbow

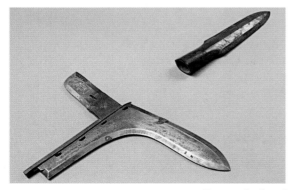

Bronze halberd

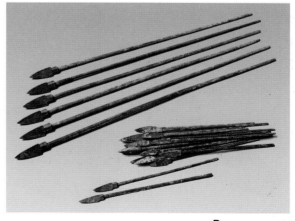

Bronze arrows

The unearthed weapons demonstrate that Chinese metallurgy reached a high level in the Qin Dynasty. The Qin weapons were even standardized made then. Analysis has shown that the pointed heads of the bolts are triangular cones with equal sides. The two bolts on all the crossbow triggers are interchangeable. The arms manufacturing industry was well developed and strictly administered by the Qin State, too. A number of excavated weapons from the terracotta pits have brief inscription, describing the name of official unit for manufacturing arms. We can believe that the most advanced technology and top craftsmen of that era were involved in creating these brilliant bronze weapons.

Bronze spear with inscription

Crossbow trigger

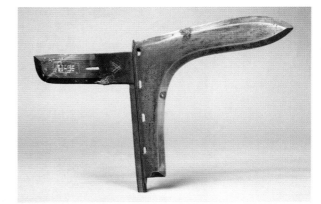

Bronze dagger with inscription

The Restoration of Terra-cotta Figures and the Preservation of Colored Warriors

According to ShiJi (Records of Historians), XiangYu, a rebel in the Qin Dynasty, burnt Emperor Qin's palace and his mausoleum in 206 BC. So the construction of the pits was damaged during the fire. The collapsed roof pressed the terra-cotta warriors and horses into fragments. None of them was completed when unearthed. Mending broken figures becomes a painstaking work for archaeological workers.

There is a company of partly assembled statues at the western end of Pit No. 1, where located the temporary restoration site of the museum now. Buried beneath them, more terra-cotta warriors and horses await to be unearthed. A group of skilled workers toil here everyday to test the missing parts and try to make the right connections. Thousands of fragments awaiting connection have lain for years in long piles on the ground. Some fragments have marks on to indicate where the item was found and to which statue it might belong, but most don't. According to the marks, the pieces were glued together by epoxy resin. Most of time, each statue would take

a few months to be mended. If the workers can find one piece that fits in a day--that will be a lucky day. The final restoration step is to patch up the statues and then they will be sent back to the original places where they were found.

Every since the terra-cotta warriors and horses were discovered 25 years ago, the flaking off of the paint has tormented archaeological experts from around the world. After years of research, two new technological methods were invented by a team of experts of the Terra-cotta Museum and further developed in co-operation with experts from the Cultural Relics Office of Bavaria of Germany since 1996. These two inventions are known as PEG200 and HEMA and now extensively applied on the newly unearthed kneeling archers from Pit 2. They can keep the original paint on the statues from fading and flaking after being brought to light. These achievements won the second prize of the National Scientific & Technological Progress Award. The museum has established the Key Scientific Research Base of Polychrome Terra-

Cotta Conservation sponsored by the State Administration for Cultural Heritage.

Archaeological experts revealed that craftsmen in the Qin Dynasty first painted a layer of lacquer on the surface of the sculptured warriors, and then colored them with paint made of minerals. The water remained in the layer of lacquer evaporated soon after the warriors being unearthed and made the paint layer get creased.

The aim of two inventions is to replace the water in the lacquer layer and keep the paint on the lacquer layer from getting creased. The experts of the museum covered the colored terracotta warriors with a solvent of PEG200, which slowly permeates into the lacquer layer to replace the water.

The other way is using a special chemical, dubbed HEMA, before stabilizing the paint by electronic beaming.

Both inventions worked, but the HEMA is now used more often than the PEG200 because experiments have revealed that it works better on large pieces than the PEG200.

Unearthed fragments of the pottery figures

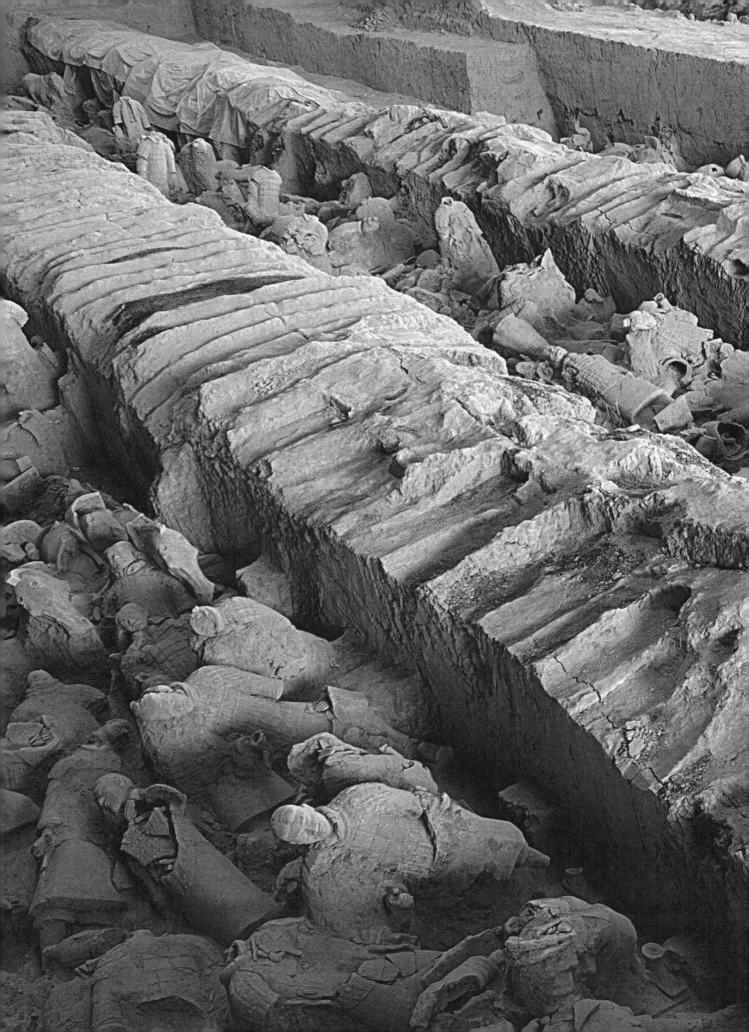

The temporary restoration site, located at the western end of Pit 1

Unearthed fragments of the pottery horses

The restoration of a pottery figure

Unearthed pottery head with a green face

The flaking off of the paint on the face of the pottery figure

Preservation at the excavated site

图书在版编目(CIP)数据

梦幻的军团=The Qin Dynasty Terra-Cotta Army
of Dreams/张琳编译. —西安：西安出版社，2005.8
ISBN 7-80712-184-X

Ⅰ.梦...　　Ⅱ.张...　　Ⅲ.秦始皇陵—简介—英文
Ⅳ.K928.76

中国版本图书馆CIP数据核字（2005）第100476号

The Qin Dynasty Terra-Cotta Army of Dreams

Author：Zhang Lin

Editor-in-chief：He An

Photographer：Xia Juxian　Guo Yan

Designer：Shaanxi HuanCheng Printing Company LTD.
　　　　　Shaanxi Dragon-Mountain Culture Spread Co., LTD.

Publisher：Xi`an Press

Address：56(N) Chang`an Rd. Xi`an

Tel：（029）85253740 85234426

Post Code：710061

Printed by Shaanxi JinPeng Printing Co., LTD

Size：889×1194　1/16

First Print：August 2005

Printing Amount：1—60,000

ISBN 7-80712 -184 -X/K · 7

Price：120.00 Yuan